The Power of
a New Attitude

Also by Doris Gothard:

SEVEN STEPS TO WEALTH

Email us at Wealthsda@DorisGothard.com or

To order, visit us at www.dorisgothard.com

for information on other products.

The Power of a New Attitude

Attitude: The Winner's Edge

Email us at Attitude@DorisGothard.com or

To order, visit us at www.dorisgothard.com

for information on other products.

The Power of a New Attitude

A POSITIVE ATTITUDE PAVES THE WAY FOR POSITIVE RESULTS!

"You are the only one who can change *your* attitude and unlock *your* potential!"
– Doris Gothard

DORIS GOTHARD

The Power of a New Attitude
Copyright @ 2011 by Doris Gothard

Printed by Lightning Source, an INGRAM Content Company

Library of Congress Control Number: 2011909380
Gothard, Doris.
Title: The power of a new attitude.

This book was
Edited by Sue Pauling
Cover Illustration by Carolyn Sheltraw
Interior Design by Carolyn Sheltraw
www.csheltraw.com
Typeset: Adobe InDesign CS5

Front Cover Photo and Photo of the Eagle inside book by Tom and Pat Leeson. Text copyright 1973 George Laycock from the book The American Eagle by Tom and Pat Leeson, reprinted with permission from Beyond Words Publishing, Hillsboro, Oregon.

Doris Gothard's Photo on Back Cover by
Photographer, Dr. Jeffery T. Baker, DDS SMILES by BAKER
www.smilesbybaker.com

Doris Gothard. — 1st ed.
A positive attitude paves the way for positive results /
    1. Self-Improvement: Motivational & Inspirational. 2. Personal Growth – Self-Esteem. 3. Personal Growth – Success.

ISBN: 9780615496498

www.DorisGothard.com

Printed in the United States of America

ABOUT THE COVER

The eagle has always been a favorite heroic image in literature
and song, as in the metaphorical imagery of biblical writers to
whom the eagle is a symbol of exalted status, youthful strength,
swiftness, farsighted vision, fierceness, freedom from earthly ties, and above all,
God's care for his children.
Thus, Isaiah writes,
"But they that wait upon the Lord
shall renew their strength;
they shall mount up with wings
as eagles …."

— *Stanwyn G. Shetler*[1]

THE POWER OF ATTITUDE - EAGLE STORY

"What Should I Do?"[2]

The nest of young eagles hung on every word as the Master Eagle described his exploits. This was an important day for the eaglets. They were preparing for their first solo flight from the nest. It was the confidence builder many of them needed to fulfill their destiny.

"How far can I travel?" asked one of the eaglets.
"How far can you see?" responded the Master Eagle.
"How high can I fly?" quizzed the young eaglet.
"How far can you stretch your wings?" asked the old eagle.
"How long can I fly?" the eaglet persisted.
"How far is the horizon?" the mentor rebounded.
"How much should I dream?" asked the eaglet.
"How much can you dream?" smiled the older, wiser eagle.
"How much can I achieve?" the young eagle continued.
"How much can you believe?" the old eagle challenged.

Frustrated by the banter, the young eagle demanded,
"Why don't you answer my questions?"
"I did."
"Yes. But you answered them with questions."
"I answered them the best I could."
"But you're the Master Eagle. You're supposed to know everything.
If you can't answer these questions, who can?"
"You," the old wise eagle reassured.
"Me? How?" the young eagle was confused.

"No one can tell you how high to fly or how much to dream. It's different for each
eagle. Only God and you know how far you'll go. No one on this earth knows your
potential or what's in your heart. You alone will answer that. The only thing that limits
you is the edge of your imagination."

The young eagle puzzled by this asked, "What should I do?"
"Look to the horizon, spread your wings, and fly."

DEDICATED

This book is dedicated with the greatest love and affection to my family and …

To God for giving me everything—life and the passion to do His work.

To my young friends,
who give their unconditional love, support and encouragement.
– Abigail, Abrianna, Allonna, Amber Lyons, Angel, Anyae', Ashlon, Ava, Aydan, Cameron, Cariel, Carmiela, Carmiya, Chanell, Cheyenne, Christina, Courtney, Diamond, Donovan, Eva-Leigh, Eve, Geniah, Gervase II (Gerger), Iman, Issabella, Jada, Jaliya, Janai, Jordyn, Joy, Kaden, Kadence, Kahlia, Kayla, Kennedy, Khloe, Kyle, Layla, LeiLani, Lindsey, Madison, Marleigh, Messiah, Nicole, Paisley, Queen, Rylie Imani, Savanna, Savonne, Shawnica, Shidiamond, Telia-Denise, and Zarya –

To the pioneers and trailblazers,
who understand The Power of a New Attitude.
– Alana, Arianna, Ashlon, Ashlyn, Beautie, Briana, Danielle, Jessica, Kara, Keona, Kiy'Ana, Leigha, Lorelle, Marquitta, Morgan, Rhonda, Shelby, Verenisse, and Wanda –

To my role models,

whom, I want to be like, when I grow up.

– Adriana, Alexis, April, Ashlon, Audrey, Brandie, Christina, Christine, Cortney, Courtney, Crystal, Danielle, Dr. Jessica, Ellie, Francis, Gabi, Grace, Izairius, Jaliyah, Jameela, Jasmin, Juliane, Kanesha, Katherine, Kitty, Kreshona, Kristyn, Lauren Nicole, Linda, Maryam, Queanna, Sam, Sharell, Siera, Tiffany, Vernesher and Atty Carmen –

To the eagles, athletes and pathfinders,

who give me their support and helping hands.

– Brian, Caleb Darensbourg, Camerin, Carl, Charles, Christopher, Clayton, CoryJr, Demetrius, Dennis, Devin Gabriel, DJ, Domonic, Jeremiah, Donovan, Donovan Rasheed Malachi, EugeneJr, Felix, Franqui II, Gavin, GlyneG III, Isaiah, Jaelen, James II, Jayden, Jaylin, Jeramiah, Jevontae', Jonathan, Jordan, Joshua, Josiah, Kaden, Kai, KJ, Kyle, LeonJr, Matthew, Michael, Myles, Reece, Ricky II, Robert, Ryan, Sam, Sameer, SamJr, Samuel III, Samuel Kelly, Semajay, Steven, Teron, Terrance Jalen (TJ), Tristan, Tristan II, Tyler, Xavier, Zachary and CharlesO IV –

My executive leaders-in-training.

To the Cast of

"I BELIEVE"

TABLE OF CONTENTS

A GIVING ATTITUDE IS THE SECRET TO ★ SUCCESS ★

INTRODUCTION

Our attitude is the key to a better life. Our attitude is something that can be controlled. Ask yourself this question: "Am I the kind of person that others enjoy being around?" Remember, people will reflect back to you, your attitude! It is my hope this book will become a family resource book—not a children's or teens', or adolescents' book only, but a book that can be used as a tool to help individuals age 7 through adult, correct bad attitude problems for any age group. Let's take a look at my attitude about success in my life.

Attitude:

- ✔ I expect to reach the goals I set for myself!

- ✔ I expect to succeed more often than fail!

- ✔ Most people are generally no smarter than me!

- ✔ There is no good reason why I can't be as successful as anyone else!

- ✔ I expect the best, and I get it!

Remember, success is not a matter of luck, but of a positive attitude. Success comes about as a result of being prepared to succeed. Take action! Think about your attitude. Learn to have an attitude of success. When you have an attitude of failure, you are whipped before you start your day.

Bad Attitude = Bad Results. Our attitude is our general outlook on life—our tone, emotions, and feelings all wrapped up into one word. When people tell you that you have a bad attitude, they are probably trying to tell you that your tone of voice and body language are sending negative vibes. Do you always think the worst or the best when confronted with a situation? Do you have a positive or a negative attitude?

Good Attitude = Good Results. Our attitude is the feeling we have toward the situation at hand; it is a disposition, a value, or a state of mind. It is how we view life as well as how we react to life's challenges. How we dress, how we stand, our posture, how we carry ourselves, and our manner of speaking say a lot about our attitude.

Life is a matter of attitudes. Our attitude determines **HOW** we experience relationships with other people. Why is attitude important? Attitude is important because it says a lot about who we really are. Our attitude should be one of patience, thankfulness, perseverance, and faith when faced with a challenge. It should be respectful, cooperative, willing, dependable, participative, and encouraging in our relationships with others. Life can be altered by altering our attitude.

According to the *Merriam Webster Dictionary*[3], the word "attitude" is defined as "an internal position or feeling with regard to something else." When we feel misunderstood, our attitude should be that of a peacemaker—reconciling, patient, and forgiving. Our attitude is a reflection of the person inside. Feed your attitude daily. Learn to develop a good attitude by dwelling on things that are *good*. When we dwell on negative thoughts, our attitude will reflect negative thoughts.

Our choices are what make us WIN or LOSE. At the moment of choice, choose to WIN! Choose positive attitudes such as saying thank you and excuse me, completing homework and chores timely, making good grades, being helpful to others, showing kindness, picking up toys, etc. Choose positive attitudes such as encouraging, loving, humble, teachable, cooperative, considerate, selfless, and loyal. Avoid bad attitudes such as rebellion, defiance, impatience, arrogance, self-centeredness, and rudeness.

I pray that this book with its illustrations will provide you with the knowledge to help you identify your good attitudes and the bad attitudes to avoid. In my journey to a new attitude as a teenager, I worked in the Alabama cotton field's as a hired day worker, picking cotton all day long and cleaning the house as a maid, for the Cobb family (see picture on next page). I was the best cotton picker and the best maid because I had a positive attitude. Recently, on a hot summer day in Alabama, members of the Cobb family and I were re-united after more than 50 years. May you also find new opportunities to be re-united with friends and inspired to serve others in your journey to a **new attitude** in life!

Doris

THE COBB FAMILY

Doris with Dian Cobb Henderson and Geneva Cobb Grisham

Good Attitudes = Good Behaviors

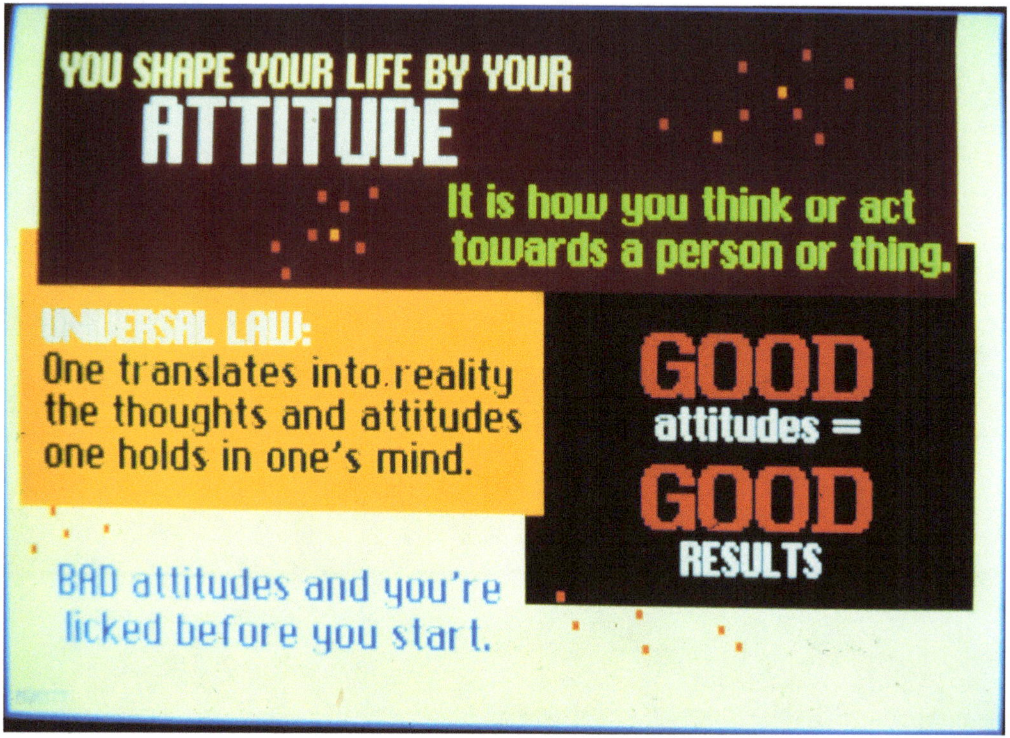

YOU SHAPE YOUR LIFE BY YOUR
ATTITUDE
It is how you think or act towards a person or thing.
UNIVERSAL LAW:
One translates into reality the thoughts and attitudes one holds in one's mind.
GOOD attitudes = GOOD RESULTS
BAD attitudes and you're licked before you start.

Good attitudes and good behaviors are demonstrated by being positive, encouraging, cooperative, etc. No one knows your thoughts, but most people can identify a person who has a good attitude. Here are some good attitude examples: "He or she is friendly and has a good attitude" or "He or she has a positive attitude."

Good Attitudes and Good Behaviors = Good Results.

Attitude

Virtually everyone remembers that one special person who earned the title of

mentor or coach because of the help he/she gave you. Maybe it was a teacher,

parent, grandparent, uncle, sister, or a neighbor. Maybe it was someone who

appreciated your potential, gave you candid feedback, or forced you to be honest

with yourself—someone who kept you on track and inspired you to go further than

you ever thought possible.

A young man named Joe chose his Uncle Don (my husband) to be his mentor

and coach. Joe is a high school principal, recently promoted to Assistant School

Superintendent in Madison, Wisconsin. Joe is currently a Ph.D. student at a

university in Madison, Wisconsin.

INSIDE STORY ❧

May 5, 2011

Thank you Uncle Don! I appreciate your steady presence and guidance in my life. I am convinced that the message of education you imprinted in our conversations over the years has been an extrinsic factor in my development. Yesterday was very intense. I had to bring a staff together who four years ago thought they would have to call in the National Guard because the school was broken and hurting. Recently, my days have been spent as a reflective and authentic instructional leader. I am spending more time on school-wide literacy and very little on eradicating gang banging in school. I have an awesome team, and we have systems in place that have gained us regional attention with community and school folks from all over visiting and writing us about how we have suppressed gang involvement in our school. I say all of this because I am ready for my next challenge. You see, people don't realize this, but other than saying something about my mother, I had better not ever hear you say, "These kids can't read or write." Those are fighting words!

It has taken me many years to realize my academic potential, and much of my inadequate feelings were influenced by the relationships and expectations of the adults around me. In my new position I will have the opportunity to ensure that all of our graduates are equipped with speaking, listening, reading, writing and reasoning skills...all kids.

So, enough of my manifesto. Our daughter Gabi is playing in a volleyball tournament in Grand Rapids this weekend. We are leaving around noon tomorrow (this is only my second tournament, so your advice was spot on). Hopefully the weather cooperates because we are going to stop at Notre Dame. I want my kids to walk one of the most beautiful and historic universities in the world. They also know that I am proud of you and your accomplishments as a student and alumnus.

Have a great day, and my best to Doris.

Love,

Joe

Here is a picture of our nephew Joe, his wife Mary,
and their children Grace (11), Gavin (8) and Gabi (14).

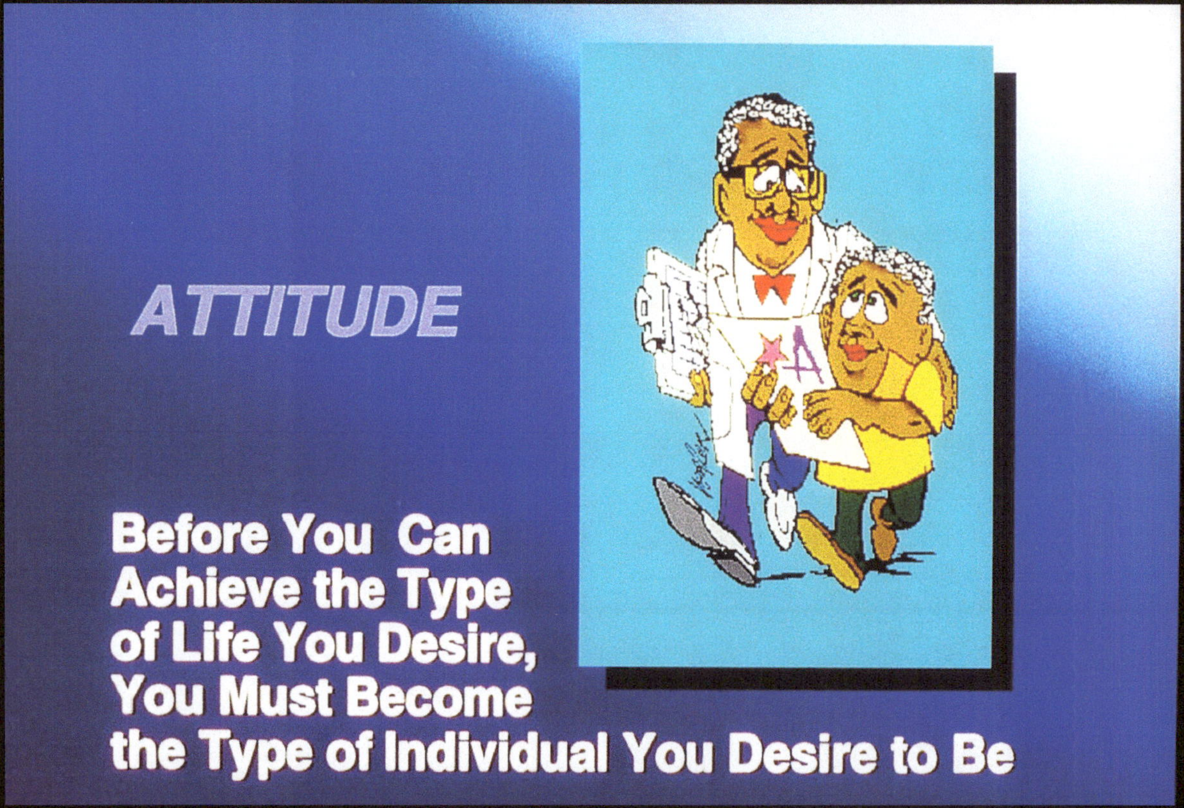
ATTITUDE
Before You Can Achieve the Type of Life You Desire, You Must Become the Type of Individual You Desire to Be
A

My nephew Gervase is the mentor for his younger brother Marcus.

My nephew Marcus is now the mentor for his nephew Terrance Jalen (TJ), Gervase's oldest son.

Choose a mentor or a coach, like Joe, to help you achieve your goals in life.

Join the Attitude NBA Team: **N**othing **B**eats **A**ttitude! Know who YOU are

and what YOU want in life, and good things will start happening for you, too.

Joe learned to think, act, talk, walk, and conduct himself as would the person he wished to become. What makes Joe's story so important? Joe is our nephew, and we are so proud of him. Joe learned from his uncle Don that hard work, preparation, and a good attitude are the keys to success.

If you believe you will succeed, you will succeed. Try to avoid focusing on your failures. Always expect to succeed more often than fail. Think positively. Expect to reach your goals. Choose a mentor or a coach to help you achieve your goals. Expect the best, and you'll get it! **NBA** - **N**othing **B**eats **A**ttitude!

You, and only you, are in charge of your attitude! A great attitude will propel you forward. There is very little difference in most people, but that little difference makes a BIG difference. The LITTLE difference is *attitude*. The BIG difference is whether you have a *good* attitude or a *bad* attitude. Choose to have a good attitude by being positive, encouraging, loving, humble, teachable, cooperative, considerate, selfless, loyal, and persevering.

Roger Van Oech in his book *A Whack on the Side of the Head*[6] wrote that people have certain attitudes that "lock" their thinking into the status quo and keep them asking for more of the same. He called them "mental locks." You can break the habit by preparing yourself to make good, educated decisions. The key to unlocking mental locks is to choose the right attitude.

As a teenager, our son LeWayne (p. 17) had *mental locks* during his teenage and young adult years. He made all the wrong choices as a teenager and young adult. But, the "sleeping giant" woke-up and unlocked the mental locks.

He changed his attitude. LeWayne made a decision to go back to school and finish his college education. We are proud of our son, LeWayne, who is now a college graduate. He is an example of a young man who changed his bad behaviors and received good results.

Nothing Beats Attitude!

Our son LeWayne, proud college graduate.

Our only grandson Justin, an automotive design college student.

Your attitude determines

HOW

you experience the world.

Bad Attitudes = Bad Behaviors

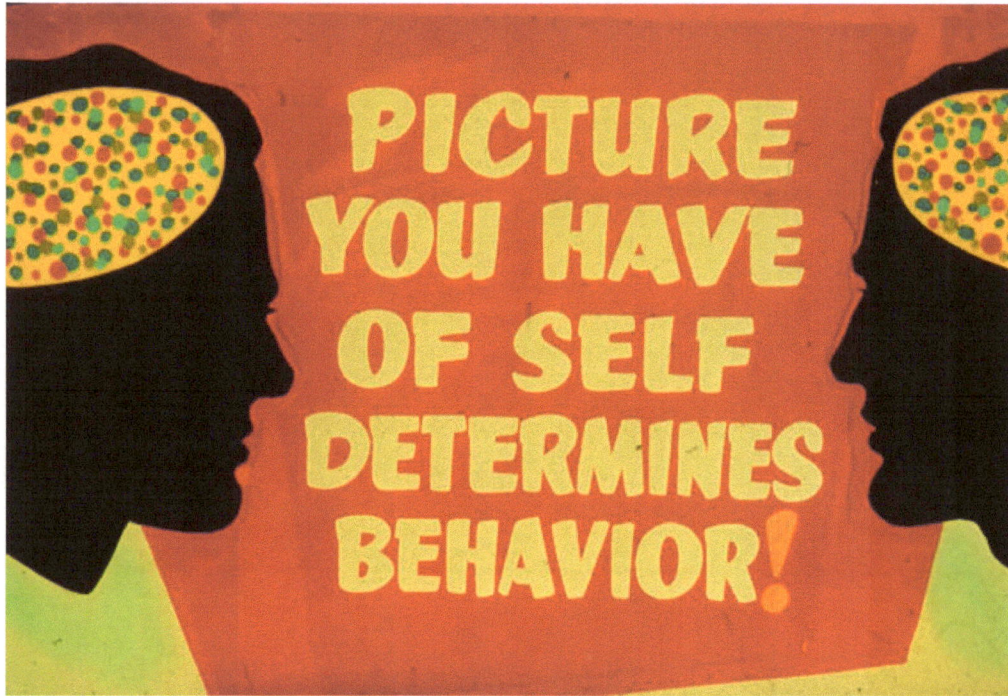

Bad Attitudes = Bad Behaviors! Most people can easily identify **bad attitudes** in

other people.. When your peers exhibit outward displays of bad behaviors such as

"I can cheat on this test" or "I can spend all this money on myself"—these are

examples of bad attitudes and bad behaviors to avoid—cheating and selfishness.

PEERS who exhibit these types of displays are persons, encouraging, errors,

rudeness and stupidity, an expression attributed to Dr. Ben Carson. Don't mimic the

bad attitudes and bad behaviors of your PEERS.

There is a lasting and powerful influence our behaviors have on our attitudes. Use your attitude to influence good behavior. Spend time with people such as teachers, coaches, parents, grandparents, uncles, sisters, friends, or neighbors who encourage and help you stay on track. There is power in your behavior.

THE POWER OF BEHAVIOR

It is amazing how our attitude influences our behavior. Our attitude makes a powerful effect on our relationships with other people by our responses, actions, reactions, conduct, and deportment. From the time we are born, our attitude has the power to either bring us closer to others or push them away from us. When we change our attitude, we change our behavior and our relationships with others.

Remember the Equation:
Bad Attitudes = Bad Behaviors.   Good Attitudes = Good Behaviors

When it comes to attitude, a picture is worth a thousand words. How people perceive you visually is more powerful than what people hear you say verbally. Everyone is responsible for his/her own actions. There is power in your attitude.

Your attitude can be used to improve the attitudes of other people. There are ways you should change your attitude to do things differently. You can make a BIG difference in someone else's life when you change your old attitude to a *new attitude*. When you change your attitude, you change your world. *That's power*!

Attitude shows a lot in how we dress. The clothes you wear say a lot about your attitude. If you want to achieve success in life, your attitude about dress is very important! Your dress is how you perceive success and failure that makes the difference in your attitude. When you have an attitude of self-confidence and self-respect, it will affect what others think about you. Here are ten decisions people make about YOU—from YOUR dress. They form an opinion about your …

1. Environment
2. Education
3. Trustworthiness or Untrustworthiness
4. Job Title
5. Prestige

6. Status
7. Culture
8. Integrity
9. Attitude
10. Success

Your attitude is either your <u>best</u> friend or your <u>worst</u> enemy, your greatest <u>asset</u> or your greatest <u>liability</u>. If someone says,

- "He has a poor attitude."

- "She is dressed inappropriately."

- "He has to change his attitude or else."

- "Her attitude is positive."

- "Her negative attitude towards her work assignment makes her uncooperative."

- "They do as they like because of their attitude."

- "They don't associate with those people because of their attitude toward them as a group."

When these things are said about you .....

YOUR ATTITUDES ARE SHOWING

Everyone is influenced by other people. The influences can be both negative and positive. Each day we associate with people who influence our attitudes in a manner similar or acceptable to themselves. The influence of a social group can affect the attitude of any individual.

Have you had someone coerce you to DO something you did not want to do that led you to such things as drinking alcohol, using drugs, smoking, or getting in trouble with the law and your parents? If the answer is yes, here is "Your Attitude is Showing Equation":

Bad Behavior = Bad Results.

Have you ever had someone convince you NOT to do something were planning to do, and it turned out well? If the answer is yes, here is "Your Attitude is Showing Equation":

Good Behavior = Good Results.

The good attitude equation can benefit you by helping you learn something, avoid breaking the law or getting into trouble with your parents, have a new experience, overcome fear and find new friendships, encouragement and good advice. It also helps define who you are and how you feel about things going on in your life.

My nephew Marcus has a good attitude. He made good choices. He finished high school with honors, received the Governor's Academic Scholarship Award, went to college, and graduated from a university in Georgia. Today, Marcus is a Technical Support Specialist in Atlanta, Georgia, employed by the largest technology services provider in the world. He found his best friend and asked her to marry him.

Right Attitude and Right Choices = Good Results.

My nephew Marcus and his beautiful wife Mayelyn.

PEERS who display negative attitudes can encourage bad attitudes in other people. Some examples are as follows: "He was showing some attitude during class today, so the teacher sent him to the office" "You need to change your bad attitude" "I don't know what the problem is, but she has a real attitude." When we allow people with bad attitudes to be a part of our lives, we allow their bad attitudes to become our attitude. **Bad Attitudes = Bad Behaviors.**

Perception is everything! People tend to reflect back to you – the attitude they see in you. Whether you're in elementary school, high school, college or already working as an adult, proper dress paves the way for a clear path in leadership. Any display in our dress perceived as disrespectful is RUDE. You wouldn't want to miss out on a job opportunity or not be selected for a training program that would help you become an officer in the world's strongest fighting force just because someone perceived your attire to be inappropriate.

PERSONS

The key to dealing with a bad attitude is self-confidence. Every PERSON should

avoid unpleasant outcomes at all costs. Learn to be yourself and make your own

decisions, regardless of what others think. Listen to your gut. Hang with people who

feel the same way you do. If a situation feels dangerous, learn to feel comfortable

saying "no." The most important decision is how you chose to react. Learn to make

good choices. Your attitude may seem trivial now, but you wouldn't want to lose a

friend or job opportunity simply because someone didn't like your attire.

Make sure your friends are not always encouraging you to display distracting

behaviors.

ENCOURAGING

There is an old saying that "birds of a feather flock together." This quote originates from the idea of the ancient Greek philosopher Democritus (c. 460 BC) who stated, "Creatures flock together with their kind, doves with doves, cranes with cranes and so on."[4]

Robert Half is quoted as saying: "If birds of a feather flock together, they don't learn enough."[5] The message is this: Learn as much as you can in life. Diversity among your peers and friends is what makes you strong and increases your opportunity to learn more from others. You can learn from others who may be unlike you in terms of their ethnicity, race, or religion. The key is to avoid hanging with persons who encourage negative behaviors.

Associate with people who have the same high standards as you do. Develop friendships with people who will help keep you are on the right course. Mistakes will happen. Some mistakes can be corrected. But something made wrong and left wrong is an **error** – in need of correction such as a misspelled word in writing, inappropriate choices of peers, or bad behaviors. You are the only person who has the power to avoid mistakes when choosing your peers. Avoid **errors** in your associations with others.

If you are dressing for a job interview, follow these simple guidelines:

- Women should wear a simple hair style, suit or dress or matching jacket, neutral-colored sheer hose, simple pumps, and a minimum of makeup; this is typical attire required for a job interview, meeting or workplace.
- Men should wear a conservative suit or slacks and jacket, white shirt, contrasting tie, shined shoes, matching belt and over-the calf socks. This is typical attire required for a job interview, meeting or workplace.

Always dress for success. Dress appropriately for every occasion. Learn to be respectful in your attitude about dress.

RUDENESS

Here is a picture of my two nieces who are straight "A" students and dress appropriately for every occasion. Jaliyah (14) left and Ashlon (16) right.

Always inquire about the proper dress code for each occasion. Rudeness in ones dress is inherently disruptive. Rudeness in ones dress for any activity is always disruptive! Organized outdoor activities such as band, train leaders to lead and dress appropriately. Some school programs offer tuition assistance by granting numerous scholarships to members who qualify. Youth oriented school programs provide education and leadership development training to high school students through programs that inspire youth to be problem solvers, decision makers, and future leaders in their communities. Consider connecting with a group of instrumental musicians in an outdoor school marching band or join a program to develop the next generation of technology and leadership. That's the *winner's edge!*

Stupidity shows a lack of intelligence. Avoid outward displays in your actions which are distracting to others. Choose to think, talk, act, walk, dress, and conduct yourself appropriately. In every circumstance, you can choose your attitude!

SELF-TALK
I'm going to change, learn, and improve from this.
I'm really excited about this opportunity.
I'm proud to see new developments in my growth.
Every contact with another person is a learning experience.
I feel a greater depth in myself today.
The future holds GREAT THINGS in store for me!
I am creative and innovative.
SELF-TALK

Self-Talk

EFFECTIVE SELF-TALK
SHORT sentences.
POSITIVE statements.
Don't have to be true NOW!
(Mostly just truth in advance)
Reflect what you WANT to be true
Speak OUT LOUD to yourself.

SELF-TALK is influenced by a verse in the Bible from Proverbs 23:7 (KJV), "For as he thinketh in his heart, so is he." When you wake up in the morning, what thoughts are on your mind? Our attitude, thoughts, outlook on life, the way we dress, and the language we use have an impact on other people.

Here is a story about a father and his two sons[7]. The wise father wanted to teach his sons a valuable lesson about life. One morning he took them on a long hike around the lake near their home. Before they left the house, the father instructed the boys to bring their backpacks.

"I am conducting an experiment, boys," said the father. "So don't ask any questions until we get home, and I will explain." The boys agreed.

From time as they walked along the country road, the father would bend down pick up a rock and place it in one of their backpacks. At another point, the father would stop for a moment take a rock or two from out of one or both boys' backpacks. This same scenario continued throughout the day. Finally, just before sunset, the boys and their father returned home. When they reached the house, the two boys were tired. Their backpacks were heavy with a variety of rocks, and they were thankful that they didn't have to carry them on their backs anymore.

Now, warm and comfortable, sitting on their family-room couch, one boy asked, "Dad, can you tell us now about your experiment?" The boys were curious, probing, "Why did you keep putting rocks in our backpacks and then take some out?"

The father explained that when he was young, his dad conducted this experiment with him, and he has always remembered its important lesson. "Today," the father explained, "I gave you both an attitude test."

The boys questioned, "What? What's an attitude test?"

The father replied, "As we were hiking, I was listening carefully to everything you two boys said, and whenever one of you complained or spoke negatively about a person or a situation, I picked up a rock and put it in your backpack."

The boys stared at each other wide-eyed, with a confused look on their faces. Continuing, the father said, "But, when either of you displayed a grateful, generous attitude, when you spoke of the best in others or a belief in yourself, I removed a rock from the bag."

After 60 seconds of complete silence, the father asked his sons to take a look at the backpacks they had been carrying all day. "Wrong thinking, regrets, frustrations, and unforgiveness are like those rocks. You can hold them in your mind, just like you carried them in your backpack," the father said. "If your mind becomes too cluttered with discouragement, it can prevent great things from happening in your future." The father hugged his boys and concluded, "Always remember the power of a positive attitude. Pay attention to your thoughts. Listen to the words you use, and notice how you say them."

We must choose wisely, not permitting destructive, toxic thoughts to rule our minds. The Bible tells us in Colossians 3:2 (NIV), "Set your minds on things above, not on earthly things." Attitude is everything. When attitudes go down, our potential goes down with it. When attitudes go up, our potential goes up too.

Choose your attitude. Wake up every morning expecting the best out of your day, and you will get it. Dream big! Rise above challenges with a positive attitude. Claim the right to choose a positive attitude every day and unlock your potential to live a victorious and successful life. Wake up each morning and do some attitude: **SELF-TALK!**

Your ATTITUDE ATTITUDE ATTITUDE ATTITUDE **is the one thing you have totally under your control.**

You may not be able to:

- **control inflation, but how you view it is up to you.**

- **avoid having a flat tire, but how you think about it is your choice.**

ALL YOUR LIFE YOU WILL HAVE PROBLEMS, BUT EVERY PROBLEM HAS A......

SOLUTION

Choose
Your Attitude

Learn a new skill.

Choose a role model.

Not everything is fair in the real world. Not all environments are accepting of

differences in people. Life is not always about race, color, hair or sex. When some

people achieve more than others, it's more about having a good attitude than one's

abilities that determines success in life. Choose a role model. Learn a new skill.

Look in the mirror! It's time to take charge! Your attitude is a reflection of the person

inside. You have the power to choose your attitude. Keep your mind on things that

are good. If you dwell on negative things, your attitude will reflect negative things,

and you will be whipped before you start your day. Look in the mirror. Part of the right

attitude is to develop a *"new attitude."*

It doesn't matter what we do
until we accept ourselves.
Once we accept ourselves,
it doesn't matter what we do.

People buy into your enthusiasm before they buy into you.

"Tomorrow, you promise yourself, will be different, yet,

tomorrow is too often a repetition of today."[8]

– *James T. McCay*

Choose to have a positive attitude in every circumstance.

I choose my attitude in every circumstance

Your attitude, opinions, and thoughts do matter! Only your own thoughts, words, and attitudes can hurt you. The path to a successful attitude is NOT as difficult as you might think. Each time you overcome an obstacle, your path to success becomes easier. Your attitude, will to a large degree, determine the eventual results in your life.

Say to yourself ... Success in life comes about as a result of being prepared. MY journey to a *new attitude* is one of life's privileges to me! MY success in life will come as a result of being prepared. MY success in life will not be a matter of luck, but hard work, preparation, and a positive attitude. It will take hard work to be successful in life. But - MY rewards in life will be the results of MY efforts. MY good attitude will be a continuous journey. The way I talk about myself today, creates my tomorrow. MY good attitude will help me through tough times. MY good attitude will determine the results in MY life.

We can be shaped & molded by our problems,
or we can be challenged & motivated by them.
To welcome a problem without resentment is
to cut its size in half.
We can see our setbacks as adversities or . . .
as adventures, confinements or challenges,
dungeons or doorways.
"A" is the author of many songs;
tribulation is inspiration for many poems.
"A" causes some people to break,
others to break records.

A "can-do" attitude will shape your life. In every circumstance, choose to have a

positive attitude. A poor attitude will make others miserable, including you. We are

either the masters or the victims of our attitudes. It's a matter of personal choice—

blessing or curse.

GET OUT OF YOUR OWN WAY!

Little things like weather conditions, technology, personal situations, environment, and other people can undermine your choice of attitude. The news, waiting in traffic, the doctor's office, postal service, grocery store, or airline delays can undermine your attitude. Things that break—the car won't start, the VCR won't play, the cable television network is down—can undermine your attitude. Generation differences and problems with relatives or neighbors (the way they act, the way they look) can undermine your attitude. Having to work, ailments, the past, or losing something you can't find can undermine your attitude.

Are you killing yourself with your own attitude? Choose to have a positive attitude every day. The problem is not the problem. The problem is your ATTITUDE about the problem. Choose a positive attitude for every circumstance.

ATTITUDE
The Deepest Craving of Human Beings Is to Be Needed, to Feel Important, and to Be Appreciated

Treat every contact with another person as a learning experience. There are indelible

links between the CHOICES we make and what we accomplish. Get excited about

the opportunity to choose. The future holds great things in store for you when you

make right choices in life. Make a decision to change, learn, and improve the choices

you make in life. Remember: You can choose your attitude.

When someone does something kind for you, recognize it. **Say "Thank you."** Make

others feel needed, important, and appreciated, and they will return the same to you.

A simple "thank you" goes a long way.

Everyone likes to feel that they are of value and that they count. Encouraging words are essential to life. Just as a plant needs water, we all need a little encouragement from time to time. We all make mistakes. We all need encouragement from a helping hand to help us evaluate our mistakes. An attitude of gratitude is important because attitude truly is everything! It drives virtually every decision you make and how you live each day of your life. Attitude either propels you forward or holds you back. While the external circumstances in your life can be chaotic, your attitude is the key to a better life. Are you in need of encouragement? You are not alone. Be confident. Know what you want in life.

Eli Whitney had an OPTIMISTIC attitude. Eli Whitney's invention of the cotton gin revolutionized the cotton industry in the United States. Prior to his invention, farming cotton required hundreds of man-hours to separate the cottonseed from the raw cotton fibers. Many people said his machine would put thousands of people out of work. Instead, the invention made the production of cloth much cheaper, and millions of people were able to buy more clothing, which created countless jobs.

Charles Babbage had an OPTIMISTIC attitude. Charles Babbage invented the computer. When the computer was invented, many people believed they would lose their jobs. Almost everyone will agree that computers have improved how we communicate. Part of the right attitude is to look for the good in people and be open to the ideas of others. You too can dream the impossible! You can start your own business or become an inventor.

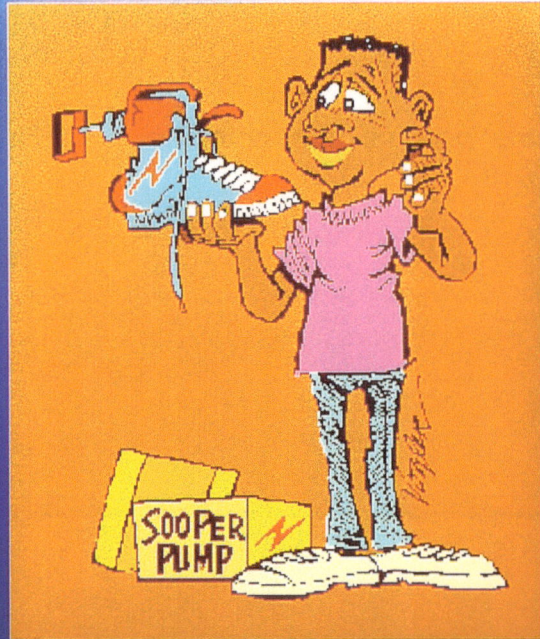

Anything can be accomplished with the right attitude. Pump up your *new attitude*

like you would pump up your "Sooper Pump, stylish, leather soft, supportive, and

comfortable" tennis shoe.

Be curious to learn more. Curiosity in new ideas is an important trait of genius.

Albert Einstein never stopped asking questions. He was curious. Curiosity builds

on the best in new ideas. Curiosity is an attitude which expands the boundaries of

our thinking. It says, "I know my assumptions about the world are incomplete, but I

want to know more." Nothing beats a good attitude. Expand the boundaries of your

thinking. Set high standards for yourself. Anything can be accomplished if you have a

positive attitude.

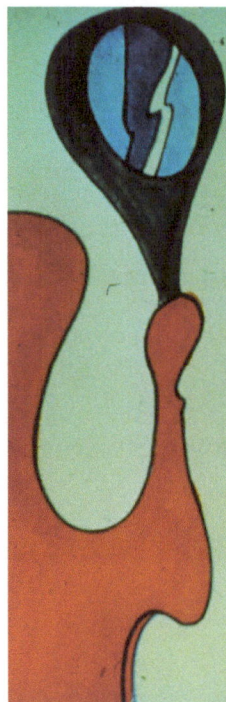

Many people succeed
when others
do not believe in them.
Rarely does a person
succeed when they
do not believe in
themselves.

Doris's friends – sisters Telia-Denise (9) and Eva-Leigh (11) (left) and Verenisse (15) (right).

If you believe you are going to fail, you will fail. If you believe you are

going to succeed, you will succeed!

You will KNOW you have the right attitude about new ideas when you can say, "I know my assumptions are incomplete, but I want to know more." Look for GOOD ideas everywhere.

Get an Attitude!

key to success in life is having an "up" spirit and a "can-do" attitude.

The most powerful force is what you say to yourself. Only our own thoughts, words, and attitudes can hurt us. Our attitude, opinions, and thoughts do matter. Never, ever feel like a failure. New opportunities lead to a new attitude. Never give up!

When faced with a challenge in life, try to discipline yourself to think positively. When your attitude is positive, you will master your difficulties. Remember: You can choose your attitude. Choose your attitude—*choose your power!* DON'T let life's challenges get you down! Learn values that will help you build a positive "can-do" attitude such as humility, curiosity, empathy, and trust. Nothing beats a failure but a try.

DON'T LET IT GET YOU DOWN

Jockey Eddie Arcaro lost his first 45 races. Michael Jordan was cut from his high school basketball team. You will not be remembered for the number of times you failed in the beginning, but for the number of times you succeeded in the end.

When you find yourself in a difficult situation, DON'T despair. Your head is your

greatest asset. The chief purpose of your body is to carry your brain around. It is your

mind, working in a calm, cool fashion that solves your problems. Failure is not the

last word! Keep your thoughts under disciplined control—no drugs, no alcohol, no

tobacco. Cultivate the right attitude that will help you succeed in the end.

Choose to see your setbacks as doorways to opportunities and adventures instead

of adversities, confinements, challenges, and dungeons. When you welcome your

problem without resentment, you can cut its size in half. You can be shaped and

molded by your problems, or you can be challenged and motivated by them.

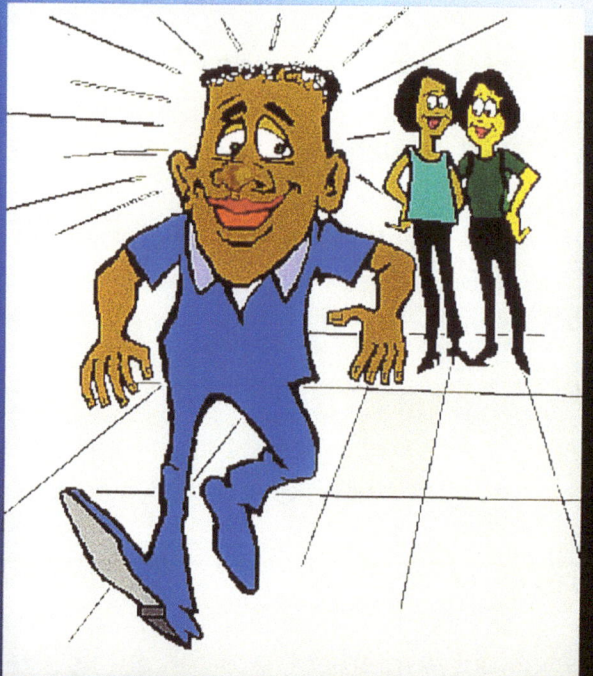

The right attitude at the beginning of your journey to a *new attitude* in life will affect the outcome MORE than anything else. Say, "Yes, I can! Yes, I will!" Since your mind can only hold one thought at a time, you should fill your mind with positive thoughts. Be willing to learn new things from others. Get really good at what you do. You are IN CHARGE. What you say, think, and do **builds confidence**! Build your confidence with a *new positive attitude.*

Walk like you matter! Radiate confidence. It is good when friends check out your *new attitude.* Now that's *power*! A negative attitude will never defeat a person with a positive attitude.

THE DRAPER FAMILY

My nephew Gervase with his wife Joanil and their sons Gervase II (Gerger on left) and Donovan.

Gervase is now a college graduate with a wife (Joanil) and three boys, Terrance Jalen (TJ), Gervase II (Gerger) and Donovan. Gervase is currently an IT Voice Analyst working for a large telephony services company in Atlanta, Georgia. Since his childhood, Gervase has always admired his Aunt Doris. Since his childhood, Gervase has always admired his Aunt Doris.

When his 7th grade teacher asked him to write a paper about a person he most admired. Here is what Gervase wrote about his Aunt Doris:

MY AUNT

I have a beautiful aunt both in spirit and in body who has smooth yellow skin accented by hazel green eyes that gleam like the stars of heaven. Her elegant clothing is always right for the occasion. She smiles a lot, so you can see the beauty of her happiness deep within her eyes. Her walk is a stride that says at all times "I Am Somebody."

What makes Gervase's Story so important? Gervase learned that the key to success is a good attitude. Gervase is our nephew, and we are so proud of him.

Make a decision to wake up every day with an attitude that says, "I am somebody. I am of value and worth, and I am going to learn something new today and live my life fully and joyfully."

Your attitude, more than anything else, will determine your success or failure. It is your **attitude** that will determine your **altitude** in life. For the rest of your life, expect the best and get it! Man is the only known creature who can reshape and remold himself by altering his attitude. Your attitude is important.

Very little is needed to make for a happy life when you have good health, family, friends, and a positive attitude. Feed your attitude daily. Learn to develop a good attitude by dwelling on things that are good. When we dwell on negative thoughts, our attitude will reflect negative thoughts. Our attitudes are intertwined with the roles we try to play in life…how we see ourselves, how we really are, and how others see us.

A life without prayer is like a computer without the software. Life without prayer is life without HOPE. Life without prayer is boring and empty. Prayer is like a passion for something to come true that seems impossible to do. PRAYER is a good thing. It is the force that energizes our faith every day!

The greatest privilege God gives to us is the freedom to approach Him at any time. Trouble and perplexity drive us to prayer, and prayer drives away trouble and perplexity. Nothing can tilt things more dramatically in our favor than prayer! Prayer changes things! When we depend upon man, we get what man can do; when we depend upon prayer, we get what God can do.

TODAY, OUR WORLD EXISTS BECAUSE OF
TOMORROW WILL GROW FROM
CHOICES
WE MADE YESTERDAY
YOU AND I MAKE TODAY!

Choose
Your Friends

THE LYONS FAMILY
"Making CHOICES is a family affair."

Jordan, Kelly (Mother), Camerin and Elliott (Father) says "It is a privilege to be involved in our sons lives to help them make right CHOICES in life." Both Jordan and Camerin are good students, good athletes and good citizens because their CHOICES are a Lyons family affair.

At a teen girls retreat group setting – 250 teen girls were encouraged to make right choices, build positive relationships with one another, and make new friends.

There is power in your CHOICE to choose your friends. A friend is a person who sticks closer than a brother or sister. Friends can be good as well as bad. Choose friends who encourage positive attitudes.

PEERS

Don't Waste Your Time Discussing Personal Problems

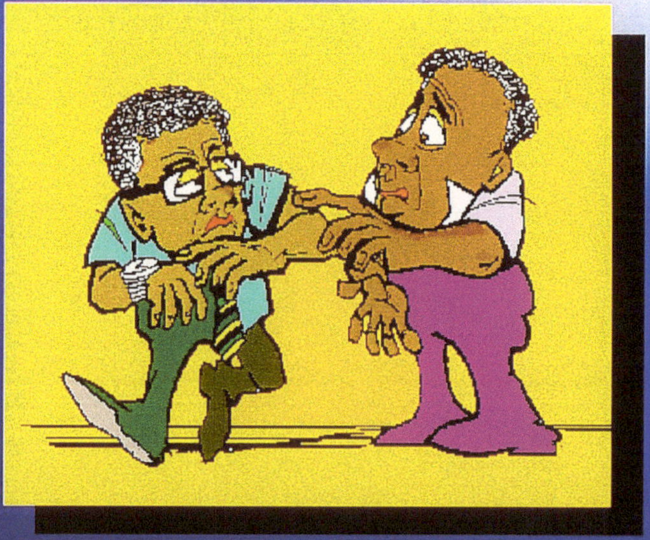

Our friends are important in our lives, but try not to waste too much time sharing too much personal information with friends who can't solve your problem. What affects them the most is our attitude. Avoid talking about serious personal problems with anyone who can't solve your problem.

Use the power of your CHOICE to choose your friends very carefully. Choose people you can learn more from and who can be positive role models. Learn to demonstrate positive attitudes and a manner of conducting yourself positively at all times. Learn to develop positive relationships with people who yearn to learn. Learn to make your own decision, regardless of what another person is encouraging you to do. Listen to your gut. Feel comfortable saying "no."

WE TEND TO ACCEPT IDEAS THAT REINFORCE OUR ATTITUDES !
– PEOPLE AND THINGS +
– WAY OF LIVING +
– MONEY & VALUE +
– JOB & WORK +
– GOALS & AMBITIONS +
– RELIGION & CHARITY +
– RIGHT & WRONG +
– POLITICS +

There is an old saying "a friend sticketh closer than a brother." Both friends and peers (based on societal groups, age, grade, status, etc.) are a part of our daily lives. Our peers are persons among our age group with whom we associate. Can you trust your peers? A friend is a person, regardless of his/her age, whom you can *trust*.

The question is this: "Do you know the difference between your peers and your friends when it comes to trust? And does it really matter? Yes. It really does matter! There is a difference, and there are times when you need to know that difference.

Develop positive relationships with friends who feel the same way you do. In other words, hang with peers who have the same positive attitude. There is power in choosing friends who encourage you not to exhibit bad attitudes. What affects other people the most is **your attitude**. Choose friends who display positive attitudes towards others.

By the same token, learn how to respond to negative peer pressure by being self-confident. Don't hesitate or be afraid to ask for an adult's help in any situation that makes you feel uncomfortable.

Doris's friend Jasmin is a mentor to her friend Lei Lani.

Doris's goddaughter Lindsey is a mentor to her little cousin Kadence.

When cars run low on oil, we add a quart of motor oil. When you feel like you are running low on *attitude* – add a quart. Become a mentor! It is an awesome responsibility! Becoming a mentor is like adding a quart of *attitude*. When you add a quart of *attitude,* you unlock your potential. Remember – you are the only one who can change your attitude.

ATTITUDE

Overcome Negative Thinking or Negative Mental Attitudes

Doris's friends Telia-Denise (left), Iman, Eva-Leigh, and Jordyn (right) are friends with a smile and positive attitude to help brighten someone else's day during their walk outside for a little exercise.

Left to Right: Friends Eva-Leigh (11), Iman (9), Jordyn (9) and Telia-Denise (9) relax outside after their walk to brighten the rest of their day!

When a friend or a peer tries to rain on your parade, you can still enjoy the rest of the day. Focus on the positive! You will see sunshine, not rain. Even our cars run low on motor oil, and we have to add a quart of oil sometimes.

FAILURE

NEED NOT BE
DISGRACEFUL
IS PROOF OF ONE'S
HUMANNESS
IS NOT
FINAL
IS NEVER
TOTAL
CAN BE
FRUITFUL

When you feel some people don't like you and are always trying to rain on your parade, nothing will be gained by holding on to this negative thought. Choose the right attitude. Listen to YOURSELF as you talk to yourself about hopeful things. A positive attitude can make you feel like you have sunshine, even on a rainy day. Think positively!

Nothing can stop a person with the right attitude from achieving his or her goal; nothing on earth can help a person with the wrong attitude. Don't allow anyone to *ruin* your day by raining on your parade! When some less informed person has tried to ruin your day by giving you a hard time, don't react as he or she would. Don't mimic the bad attitudes of others. Overcome negativity by thinking positively! Just smile it off! Rise above it!

A mistake is not failure. How you handle it could be.

I'm glad you caught that. You're a real help.

You're right. That's great.

You've given me a whole new slant on this.

I see it differently now.

Let's try your approach.

I made a mistake.
I was wrong. I failed.
It's my poor judgment.
I can't do this anymore.

A Mistake
Is Not
a Failure

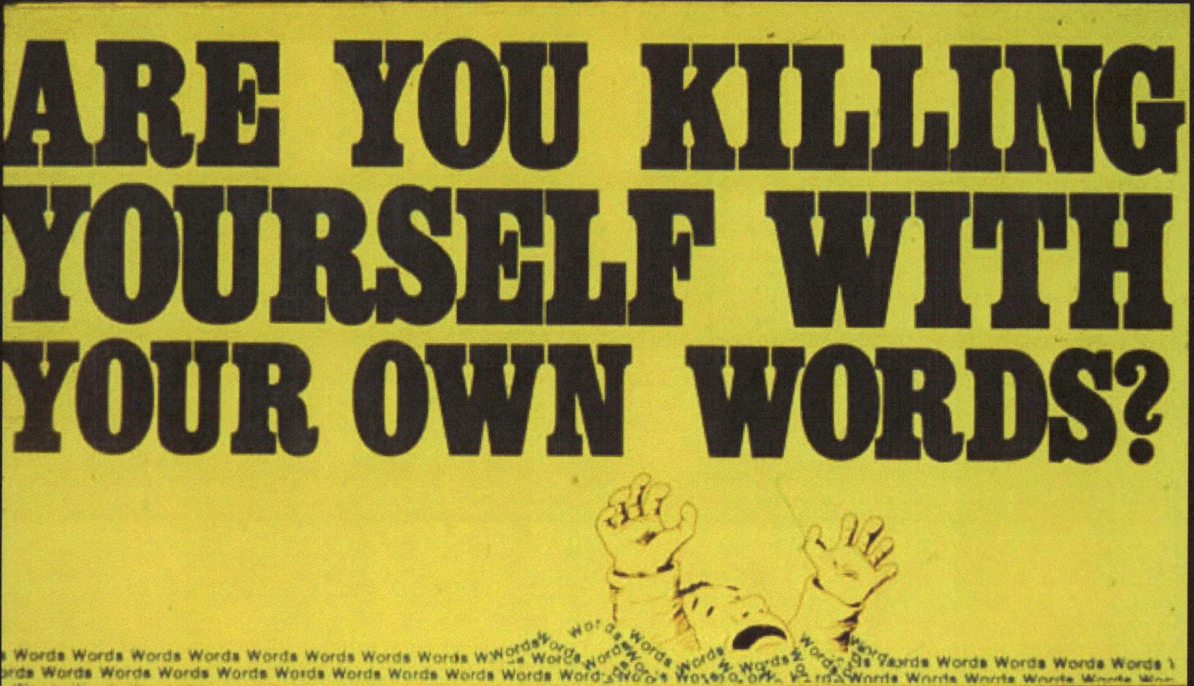
ARE YOU KILLING YOURSELF WITH YOUR OWN WORDS?

If you are afraid to face up honestly about your attitude in life, you may be afraid to

see YOU as you really are. You can't love someone you don't know. KNOW who you

really are. It is the only way to get rid of FEAR.

attitude

- ★ Do I always do my best?
- ● Am I friendly <u>and</u> cooperative?
- ★ Do I attend to details?
- ● Am I optimistic?
- ★ Do I do <u>more</u> than <u>my</u> share?
- ● Am I well-mannered?
- ★ Do I follow <u>through</u>?
- ■ Am I believable?

Feed your attitude with good thoughts daily. Learn to develop good attitudes by dwelling on things that are good. If you dwell on negative thoughts, your attitude will reflect negative thoughts. Your attitude in life will determine your success in life. The key is to act as the person you want to become. Ask yourself the following questions:

- Do I always do my best?

- Am I friendly and cooperative?

- Do I attend to details?

- Am I optimistic?

- Do I do more than my share?

- Am I well-mannered?

- Do I follow through?

- Am I believable?

Get rid of your
FEAR of FAILURE

We don't love ourselves because we don't know ourselves. "You can't love someone you don't know." We are unaware of our remarkable potentialities.

We are afraid to face up and honestly meet ourselves for fear we might discover we are failures, and we are afraid of failure.

We are afraid to find our what kind of person we really are.

Abraham Lincoln rose from humble beginnings. He had less than a year of formal education prior to running for political office. Before becoming President of the United States, Abraham Lincoln endured a steady stream of failure and defeat. He was born into poverty. He could have quit, but he didn't. He never gave up! Here is the list of "Failures of Abraham Lincoln"[9]:

A common list of the failures of Abraham Lincoln (along with a few successes) is:

- 1831 - Lost his job
- 1832 - Defeated in run for Illinois State Legislature
- 1833 - Failed in business
- 1834 - Elected to Illinois State Legislature (**success**)
- 1835 - Sweetheart died
- 1836 - Had nervous breakdown
- 1838 - Defeated in run for Illinois House Speaker
- 1843 - Defeated in run for nomination for U.S. Congress
- 1846 - Elected to Congress (**success**)
- 1848 - Lost re-nomination
- 1849 - Rejected for land officer position
- 1854 - Defeated in run for U.S. Senate
- 1856 - Defeated in run for nomination for Vice President
- 1858 - Again defeated in run for U.S. Senate
- 1860 - Elected President (**success**)

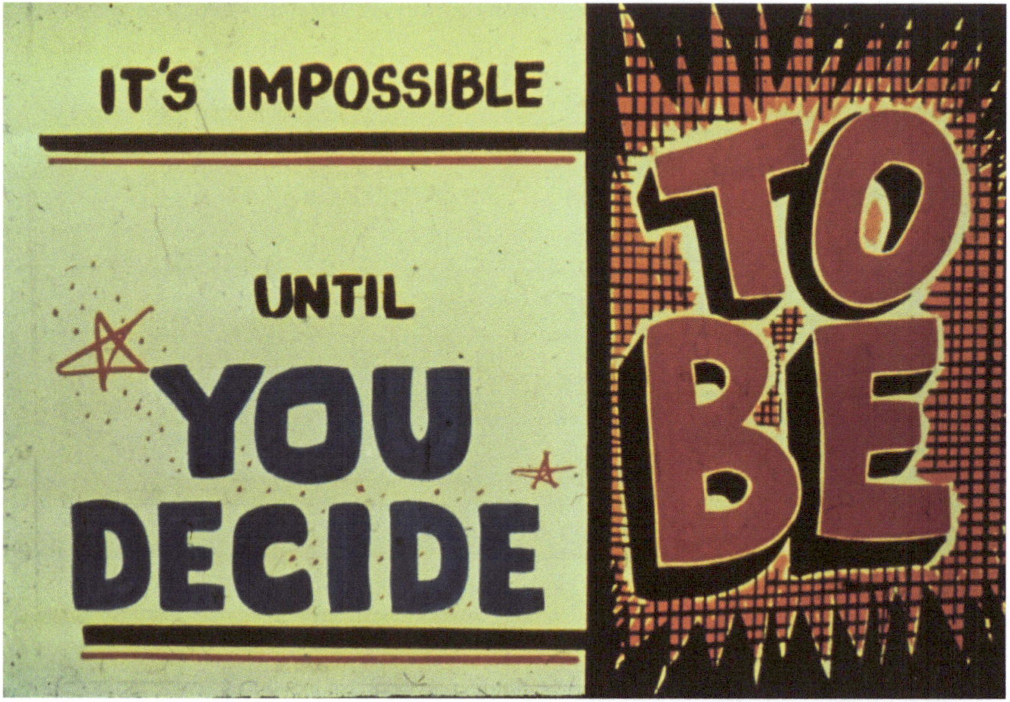
IT'S IMPOSSIBLE
UNTIL
YOU
DECIDE
TO
BE

Abraham Lincoln's resumé looks pretty glum, making you wonder how he ever made it to the top. But when you really think of it, to run for office or high positions so many times, you have to have something on the ball and have more successes than meet the eye.

Abraham Lincoln is an excellent example of *the power of a new attitude*. He never quit trying and his positive attitude for success was key to his election as the 16th President of the United States.

Thomas Edison failed thousands of times while attempting to invent the light bulb. He is reported to have said that the attempts were not failures but opportunities to know how <u>not</u> to create a light bulb. Shortly thereafter, Edison invented the light bulb. A mistake is not a failure.

Success or failure in life is determined more by our attitude than by our mental

capacities. The most powerful force is what you say to yourself.

You are the one who must bring about the results and outcomes desired in your life. Nobody else can do that for you!

The Attitude
Golden Rule

Enthusiasm is the force of God Himself energizing your body.

A 30-DAY ATTITUDE GOLDEN RULE

For the next thirty (30) days, treat everyone the way he or she wishes to be treated.

Choose to have a positive attitude and make a difference in the world. Everyday

wake-up and tell yourself – "My attitude matters!" My positive attitude is the secret

to my success today.

ATTITUDE
ATTITUDE

At beginning of task, will affect outcome **MORE** than anything else.

Radiate WELL BEING and confidence that you **KNOW** where you are going.

MAKE others feel needed, important, & appreciated, & they'll return same.

Toward life (others) **DETERMINES** life's (other's) attitude toward us.

Look for the **BEST** in all new ideas & look for **GOOD** ideas everywhere

Act "AS IF" you are the person you want to become.

Most people don't think that their attitudes matter. They wake up and react to

whatever happens to them. Don't react. Your attitude is something that can be

controlled. Your attitude determines who is rider and who is horse. You have a choice.

You either ride life or it rides you. A positive attitude is the secret to success!

Attitude! Attitude! Attitude! Remember, you have the power to choose your *attitude*.

Others will reflect back to you, the attitude you present to them.

Attitudes can be infectious. Most people want to feel recognized, appreciated and

needed. Most people want to feel that they count. When they feel these things,

they will give their love and respect, and they will buy whatever products you sell.

For the next thirty days, treat others the way they want to be treated and they will

return the favor.

Remember: Good Attitude = Good Results!

The Stages
of Your Life

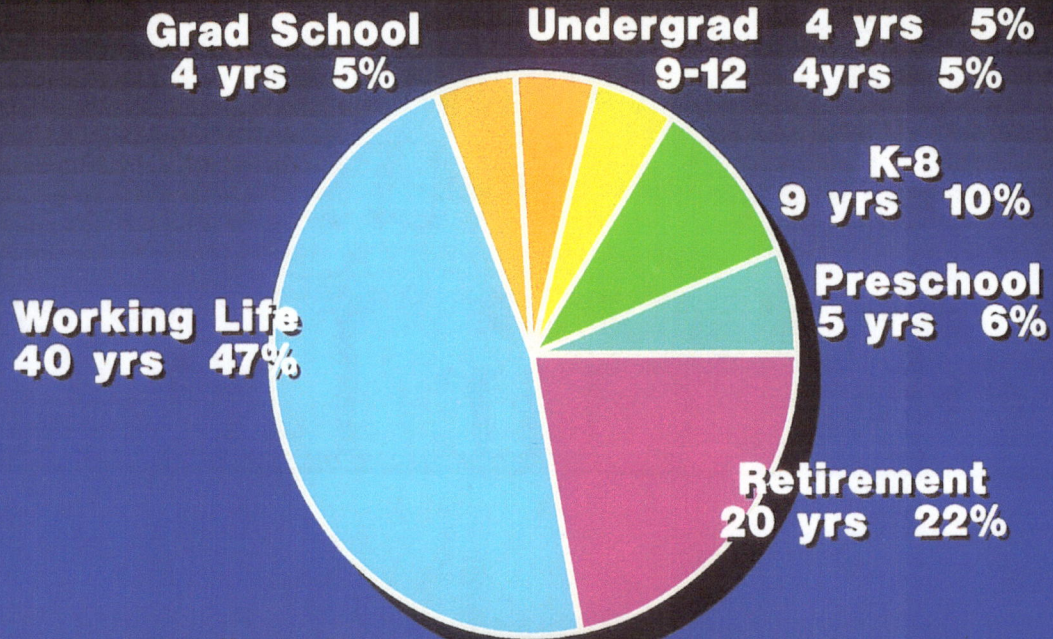

"The Stages of Life"

Written By **Donald L. Gothard**

Retired GM Executive, Washington, Michigan

Lou Holtz said it best when he said, "Ability is what you're capable of doing. Motivation determines what you do. Attitude determines how well you do it."[10]

Think about the stages of your life. Let's assume you have a life span of 86 years. You spend five years of your life at home before going to school. You spend nine years of your life in kindergarten through eighth grade. You'll then spend four years of your life in ninth grade to twelfth grade.

If you graduate from high school and go on to a college or university, you may spend four years of your life preparing yourself for a career of some sort. If you move on to graduate school to get an advanced degree, you might spend another four years of your life finishing your preparations for a future career. You might even spend five years getting your undergraduate degree and five years in graduate school getting your advanced degree. This would add another two years to your schooling. However, for this example, let's just consider that your schooling will take up 26 years or 31% of your total life.

When you have finished with your schooling, then you will begin your working life stage. Let's assume you will work until you are 66 years old before you retire. This 40-year span takes up 47% of your life. When you retire you will have a life of 20 years left, or 22% of your total life span. All together you will have a period of 60 years, or 69% of your life, remaining after educating yourself for your work and retirement years. If you do not go on to college after high school, you will have to add another eight years to your working life. Consider the kind of life you'll have if you do not prepare yourself for a working life that you should want to enjoy. Consider what the 20 years in retirement will be like if you have not prepared yourself for retirement. If you only have Social Security to provide you with income in your retirement years, you'll be living at the poverty level. It will be even worse than that if Social Security is not available to you in the future.

In conclusion, your school years are the most important years in your life to prepare you for the majority years remaining in your life after school. What all individuals must ask themselves is, "What kind of life do I want to have for the majority years of my life?" A lot will depend on what your attitude on life during your preparation years in school will be. It's up to you to make the right decisions throughout your lifetime. This book is an attempt to provide the guidelines needed to change your attitude and develop an attitude for success.

A Final Note

Dear Friends,

Attitude is everything – an idea inspired by the life and work of Dr. G. Herbert "Herb" True. Our attitude should reflect love to the members of our family and friends, forgiveness, consideration, caring, encouragement, kindness, humility, unselfishness, and respect. My final note is a note to adults (parents and teachers) because attitude should be one of patience, thankfulness, perseverance, and faith. It should be respectful, cooperative, willing, dependable, participative, and encouraging in our relationships with others. Because I was raised as a Christian, my views about attitude reflect the views expressed in Scripture and the teachings from my church. I feel very confident, however, that all of the many religions on this earth would be in support of the concepts and guidelines which I have presented in this book about good and bad attitudes. According to Scripture, our attitude should reflect the attitude of Christ: humble, loving, and trusting.

Our attitude should demonstrate obedience, cooperation, and endurance as responsible adults. It should express confidence in God's justice when we experience unfairness, disappointment, or tragedy. Our attitude should be grateful and God-glorifying, not self-exalting. Like children, when we feel misunderstood, our attitude should be that of a peacemaker—reconciling, patient, and forgiving.

My strong belief in a personal God is the foundation for my beliefs about one's attitude in life. When I became a Christian, Jesus promised to change my attitudes for the better. He promised to give me THE POWER OF A NEW ATTITUDE. I want to share a biblical principle which gave me the inspiration for writing this book.

A Biblical Principle: A New Attitude

"Therefore, if anyone is in Christ, the new creation has come: The old has gone, the new is here!" (2 Corinthians 5:17 NIV). According to Scripture, a part of our new creation is the gift of a *new attitude*. To have an attitude just like Jesus is *power!* "You were taught, with regard to your former way of life, to put off your old self, which is being corrupted by its deceitful desires; to be made new in the attitude of your minds" (Ephesians 4:22 NIV).

Our attitude is our inward disposition. "Let this mind be in you which was also in Christ Jesus" (Philippians 2:5 NIV). Our attitude should become just like Jesus: Good. What affects us most is OUR attitude toward LIFE.

"If our attitude toward life is negative, we are going to experience an unhappy world. There will always be too much traffic on the freeway, the service in the restaurant will always be too slow, our children's rooms will never be clean enough, the weather will never be nice enough, and we'll feel that family and friends should have done things better or differently. A positive attitude toward life and others is a requirement for a life of happiness. When negative situations do arise, the ability to see problems as challenges presenting opportunities for creative solutions is the difference between failure and success, unhappiness and happiness. *Do I criticize? Is my attitude positive or negative? Do my problems defeat me? Do I know that the solutions to my problems are within me?*"

    – Author Unknown

Attitude is our general outlook on life—our tone, emotion, and feelings all wrapped up into one word. When people tell us that we have a bad attitude, they are probably trying to tell us that our tone of voice and body language are sending negative vibes. Do you always think the worst or the best when confronted with a situation? Do you have a positive or a negative attitude?

Attitude affects our relationships with others. How we dress, how we stand, our posture, how we carry ourselves, and our manner of speaking say a lot about our attitude. However, Jesus has promised to give each of us a new attitude, when we allow His mind to live in us. Our *new attitude* is a matter of faith and determination to embrace God's outlook and disposition.

May you have the mind of Jesus as you use these Biblical principles to help others understand what it means to be a part of the family of God and experience "The Power of a New Attitude" as we all attempt to live Christian lives in this world. We began our journey with the joy of acknowledging the gift we receive when we become a Christian: *a new attitude*! We learned that God not only gives us a *new attitude*, but He gives us His power!

Remember, it is God who gives us the gift of a *new attitude,* and when God gives a *gift*, you deserve to have it! I pray that you have enjoyed reading this book. Thank you for taking this attitude journey with me. May you experience the power of a new attitude in your faith, courage, laughter, style, grace, charm and beauty. May you find joy in lifelong friendships with someone who is an encourager during the rough times, a supporter and helper, a confidant and best friend for life —just like my sister Roxie.

With Deepest Affection,

Doris

The Power of Friendships

Doris with her sister Roxie (right).

The Power of Friendships

Doris's great nephew, Gerger (left) had the courage to take the microphone and prove he could be the emcee of the program.
That's attitude!

Gervase II's (Gerger's) friend Liliana (right) had the courage to stand up and prove she could be a professional singer.
That's attitude!

The Power of Laughter and Beauty

Doris's brother-in-law-Pete (left) enjoys a laugh with Enrique, who told a joke with confidence. *That's attitude!*

Izairis (right) poses for a picture and shows off her style, grace, charm and beauty. *That's attitude!*

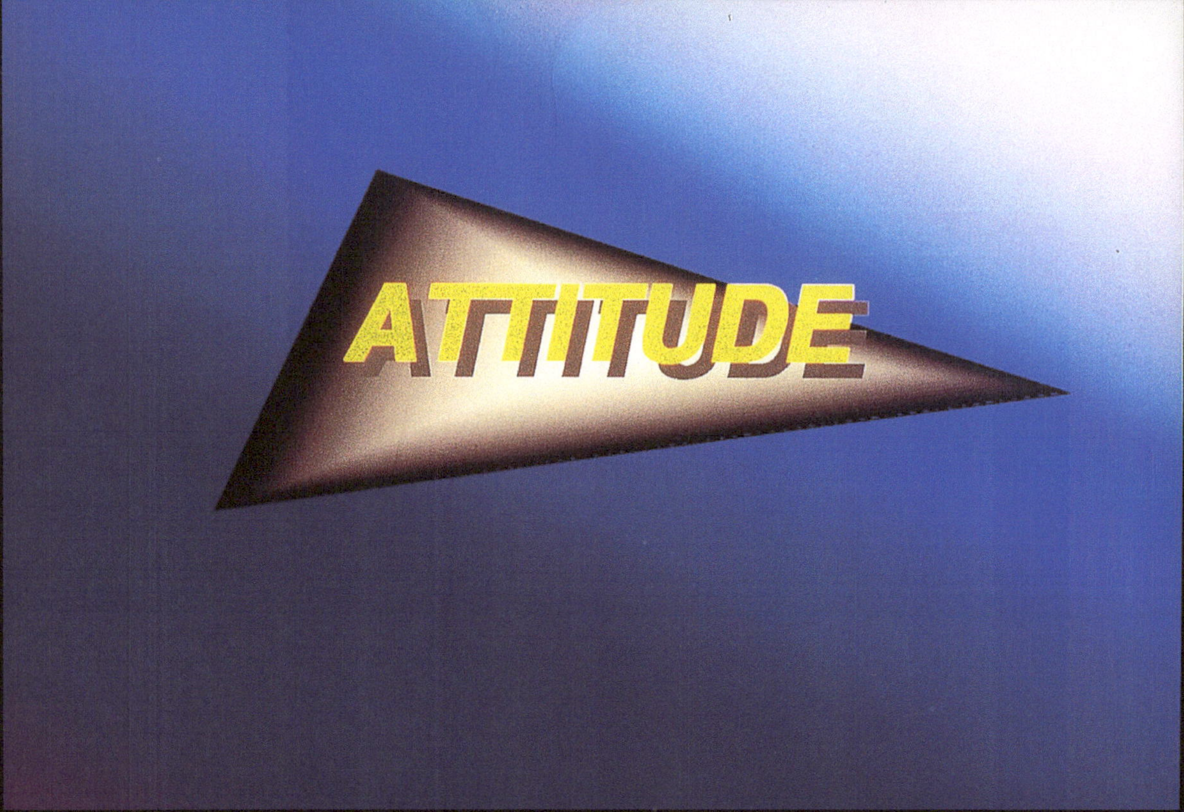
ATTITUDE

THE END

END NOTES

1. Photo by Tom and Pat Leeson. Text copyright 1973 Stanwyn G. Shetler from the book *The American Eagle* by Tom and Pat Leeson, reprinted with permission from Beyond Words Publishing, Hillsboro, Oregon.

2. Azmi, Kulshum. "The Power of Attitude - Eagle Story." *CiteHR.com.* n.d. Web. 14 May 2011. <http://www.citehr.com/206589-power-attitude-eagle-story.html>.

3. *Merriam Webster Collegiate Dictionary (11th ed.).* Springfield, MA: Merriam Webster, Inc., 2003. p.80.

4. Graham, Jerry. "Birds of a Feather." *The Coaching Pair.* 2011. Web. 14 May 2011. <http://thecoachingpair.com/blog/birds-of-a-feather>.

5. "Thoughts on the Business of Life." *Forbes.com.* 2010.Web. 14 May 2011. <http://thoughts.forbes.com/thoughts/example-robert-half-if-birds-of>.

6. Van Oech, Roger. *A Whack on the Side of the Head.* New York: Warner Books, 2008. Print.

7.   Galasso-Vigorito, Catherine. "A Great Attitude Paves the Way for Great Results." *The Macomb Daily.* 21 Jan. 2011. Web. 1 June 2011. <http://www.macombdaily.com/articles/2011/01/29/lifestyles/srv0000010662528.txt>.

8.   McCay, James T. *The Management of Time.* New York: Prentice Hall, 1995. p. 165. Print.

9.   Kurtus, Ron. "Failures of Abraham Lincoln." *School for Champions.* 11 January 2007. Web. 14 May 2011. <http://www.school-for-champions.com/history/lincoln_failures.htm>.

10.   Holtz, Lou. *Quotations Book.* 2007. Web. 14 May 2011. <http://quotationsbook.com/quote/3467/#axzz1LXho4OLV>.

www.ingramcontent.com/pod-product-compliance
Lightning Source LLC
Chambersburg PA
CBHW060803270326
41927CB00002B/34